OUR
DISHONEST
PRESIDENT

OUR DISHONEST PRESIDENT

THE *LOS ANGELES TIMES* EDITORIAL BOARD

INTRODUCTION by
Davan Maharaj and Nicholas Goldberg

Heyday, Berkeley, California

Book Design: Ashley Ingram

Orders, inquiries, and correspondence should be addressed to:

Heyday
P.O. Box 9145, Berkeley, CA 94709
(510) 549-3564, Fax (510) 549-1889
www.heydaybooks.com

Printed in East Peoria, IL by Versa Press, Inc.

10 9 8 7 6 5 4 3 2 1

Contents

Introduction

Davan Maharaj and Nicholas Goldberg *

Many Americans are nonchalant about national affairs. Even when times turn bad, we assume that this too shall pass, that the regular order of things will return shortly. A long view of history tells us that the United States has survived wars and economic depressions and political scandals, and that we shouldn't exaggerate the severity of today's threats or lapse too easily into hyperbole.

But some events are so extraordinary that they require us to put nonchalance aside. So it was with the election on November 8, 2016, of Donald J. Trump, a shallow and self-absorbed political novice whose rise to power was both unexpected and unprecedented in modern

*Davan Maharaj is publisher and editor-in-chief of the *Los Angeles Times* and Nicholas Goldberg is editor of the editorial pages.

American history, and whose dangerous tendencies set him apart from his recent predecessors.

The Trump election was a watershed that requires all of us to rise from our slumbers, to shrug off indifference, to stand up and speak out. It requires intellectual engagement, level-headed judgment and a willingness to sound the alarms. Those responsibilities fall on all citizens, but they fall especially heavily on news organizations.

The harsh, deeply disapproving six-part editorial series that is reprinted in this book was written because the *Los Angeles Times* editorial board concluded that the new president of the United States poses a threat to democracy, a threat to the institutions this country has spent hundreds of years building and a threat to America's moral standing in the world.

The series was published eleven weeks into Trump's first term. Until then, the editorial board had been writing about Trump day after day for more than a year; in the weeks after the election, we lambasted him in one-off editorials for his cabinet appointments, his executive orders, his midnight tweets, his irresponsible positions on virtually every subject he raised. We came out against his nominees for attorney general, for EPA administrator, for secretary of education.

But piecemeal, one-at-a-time editorials began to feel insufficient. It was time to take him on in a bigger, fuller way. Who was this untested, untrustworthy and impulsive president who was hiring hacks and lobbyists and corporate chieftains, surrounding himself with alt-right ideologues from the political fringes and embarking on a program to undo not just the Obama legacy, but much of the legacy of the twentieth century? Healthcare, immigration, reproductive rights, human rights, civil rights—all were on the block.

The first piece in the series—"Our Dishonest President"—was published on April 2, 2017, and it resonated instantly with readers.

That article alone was re-tweeted so often and shared so widely that within days it had been viewed more than 4.6 million times. The series overall received nearly 7 million page views. The *Los Angeles Times* got hundreds of letters and online comments and, when we opened a telephone line for responses, hundreds of calls within a two-day period. We received overwhelming praise from readers as well as angry condemnations from those who disagreed. The editorials were read not just in Los Angeles or California, but all over the country—red and blue states alike—and all over the world.

This, of course, was the best possible outcome. Editorials are supposed to take strong stands, stimulate debate, offer context and analysis, help shape people's thinking while challenging their pre-conceived notions, rigid ideologies and biases.

That's especially important at a moment when truth—our common ground for debate, dissent and accord—is being devalued. In the Trump era, facts are not only disputed, but manipulated, bent and maligned. The written word is under siege. Our most revered institutions have become objects of contempt. We live in the age of trolls, sowing discord and spreading lies. "Alternative facts" have inspired real acts of hate and retribution. "Fake news" threatens our common understanding of the world. Science itself is under attack.

This is an extraordinary challenge for newspapers and journalists, for writers and editors—and for anyone who trusts us, who turns to us for honest reports about the world.

In the Trump series, we call on citizens to vote, demonstrators to raise their banners, Republicans and Democrats alike to stand up in defense of shared American values. But newspapers like ours also have a role to play in the unfolding drama ahead. It falls to us to tell the stories of those who might otherwise become background characters on the world stage; people who are hated or ignored simply because no one has heard what they have to say or what their everyday experience is like. It falls to us to explain the complex workings of government as the new administration undoes the work of previous administrations. It falls to us to help understand and explain the president, to cut through the spin and the false narratives and the cynical misdirection.

In the weeks since the series was published, the Trump presidency has continued to flail. The president who had promised to pull back from costly overseas entanglements nevertheless launched a missile strike on Syria just three months after taking office. He dropped the "mother of all bombs" on Afghanistan. He put a conservative "originalist" on the U.S. Supreme Court. He proposed a massive tax cut that would benefit the rich above all even as he moved forward on his plan to replace the Affordable Care Act with a law that experts say could take healthcare away from at least

24 million largely lower-income Americans. Potential conflicts of interest continue to emerge, swirling around the president, his daughter Ivanka and his son-in-law Jared Kushner. In a particularly shocking and disturbing move, Trump summarily fired the FBI director who was leading the investigation into Russian interference in the 2016 election and the possibility of collusion between Russia and the Trump campaign. A week later, a special counsel was named to take over the investigation; Trump called it "the single greatest witch hunt of a politician in American history."

The United States, as we wrote in the articles collected here, is in the hands of an irresponsible, volatile and mendacious president. More than ever, we must all work to expose hypocrisy, speak up truthfully even when it is unpopular to do so and refuse to be silenced by bullies. Our nation—and the world as well—are under threat, and how we respond will define us for years to come.

OUR
DISHONEST
PRESIDENT

It was no secret during the campaign that Donald Trump was a narcissist and a demagogue who used fear and dishonesty to appeal to the worst in American voters. The *Los Angeles Times* called him unprepared and unsuited for the job he was seeking, and said his election would be a "catastrophe."

Still, nothing prepared us for the magnitude of this train wreck. Like millions of other Americans, we clung to a slim hope that the new president would turn out to be all noise and bluster, or that the people around him in the White House would act as a check on his worst instincts, or that he would be sobered and transformed by the awesome responsibilities of office.

Instead, seventy-some days in—and with about 1,400 to go before his term is completed—it is increasingly clear that those hopes were misplaced.

In a matter of weeks, President Trump has taken dozens of real-life steps that, if they are not reversed, will rip families apart, foul rivers and pollute the air, intensify the calamitous effects of climate change and profoundly weaken the system of American public education for all.

His attempt to de-insure millions of people who had finally received healthcare coverage and, along the way, enact a massive transfer of wealth from the poor to the rich has been put on hold for the moment. But he is proceeding with his efforts to defang the government's regulatory agencies and bloat the Pentagon's budget even as he supposedly retreats from the global stage.

These are immensely dangerous developments which threaten to weaken this country's moral standing in the world, imperil the planet and reverse years of slow but steady gains by marginalized or impoverished Americans. But, chilling as they are, these radically wrong-headed policy choices are not, in fact, the most frightening aspect of the Trump presidency.

What is most worrisome about Trump is Trump himself. He is a man so unpredictable, so reckless, so petulant, so full of blind self-regard, so untethered to reality that it is impossible to know where his presidency will lead or how much damage he will do to our nation. His obsession with his own fame, wealth and success, his determination to vanquish enemies real and imagined, his craving for adulation—these traits were, of course, at the very heart of his scorched-earth outsider campaign; indeed, some of them helped get him elected. But in a real presidency in which he wields unimaginable power, they are nothing short of disastrous.

"It is impossible to know where his presidency will lead or how much damage he will do to our nation."

Although his policies are, for the most part, variations on classic Republican positions (many of which would have been undertaken by a President Ted Cruz or a President Marco Rubio), they become far more dangerous in the hands of this imprudent and erratic man. Many Republicans, for instance, support tighter border security and a tougher response to illegal immigration, but Trump's cockamamie border wall, his impracticable campaign promise to deport all 11 million people living in the country illegally and his blithe disregard for the effect of such proposals on the U.S. relationship with Mexico turn a very bad policy into an appalling one.

———

In the following chapters, *The Times* editorial board will look more closely at the new president, with a special attention to three troubling traits:

1. **Trump's shocking lack of respect** for those fundamental rules and institutions on which our government is based. Since January 20, 2017 he has repeatedly disparaged and challenged those entities that have threatened his agenda, stoking public distrust of essential institutions in a way that undermines faith in American democracy. He has questioned the qualifications of judges and the integrity of their decisions, rather than acknowledging that even the president must submit to the rule of law. He has clashed with his own intelligence agencies, demeaned government workers and questioned the credibility of the electoral system and the Federal Reserve. He has lashed out at journalists, declaring them "enemies of the people," rather than defending the importance of a critical, independent free press. His contempt for the rule of law and the norms of government are palpable.

2. His utter lack of regard for truth.

Whether it is the easily disprovable boasts about the size of his inauguration crowd or his unsubstantiated assertion that Barack Obama bugged Trump Tower, the new president regularly muddies the waters of fact and fiction. It's difficult to know whether he actually can't distinguish the real from the unreal—or whether he intentionally conflates the two to befuddle voters, deflect criticism and undermine the very idea of objective truth. Whatever the explanation, he is encouraging Americans to reject facts, to disrespect science, documents, nonpartisanship and the mainstream media—and instead to simply take positions on the basis of ideology and preconceived notions. This is a recipe for a divided country in which differences grow deeper and rational compromise becomes impossible.

3. **His scary willingness to repeat alt-right conspiracy theories**, racist memes and crackpot, out-of-the-mainstream ideas. Again, it is not clear whether he believes them or merely uses them. But to cling to disproven "alternative" facts; to retweet racists; to make unverifiable or false statements about rigged elections and fraudulent voters; to buy into discredited conspiracy theories first floated on fringe websites and in supermarket tabloids—these are all of a piece with the Barack Obama birther claptrap that Trump was peddling years ago and which brought him to political prominence. It is deeply alarming that a president would lend the credibility of his office to ideas that have been rightly rejected by politicians from both major political parties.

Where will this end? Will Trump moderate his crazier campaign positions as time passes? Or will he provoke confrontation with Iran, North Korea or China, or disobey a judge's order or order a soldier to violate the Constitution? Or, alternately, will the system itself—the Constitution, the courts, the permanent bureaucracy, the Congress, the Democrats, the marchers in the streets—protect us from him as he alienates more and more allies at home and abroad, steps on his own message and creates chaos at the expense of his ability to accomplish his goals? Already, Trump's job approval rating has been hovering in the mid-thirties, according to Gallup, a shockingly low level of support for a new president. And that was before his former national security advisor, Michael Flynn, offered to cooperate with congressional investigators looking into the connection between the Russian government and the Trump campaign.

"Those who oppose the new president's reckless and heartless agenda must make their voices heard."

On Inauguration Day, we wrote that it was not yet time to declare a state of "wholesale panic" or to call for blanket "non-cooperation" with the Trump administration. Despite plenty of dispiriting signals, that is still our view. The role of the rational opposition is to stand up for the rule of law, the electoral process, the peaceful transfer of power and the role of institutions; we should not underestimate the resiliency of a system in which laws are greater than individuals and voters are as powerful as presidents. This nation survived Andrew Jackson and Richard Nixon. It survived slavery. It survived devastating wars. Most likely, it will survive again.

But if it is to do so, those who oppose the new president's reckless and heartless agenda must make their voices heard. Protesters must raise their banners. Voters must turn out for elections. Members of Congress—including and especially Republicans—must find the political courage to stand up to Trump. Courts must safeguard the Constitution. State legislators must pass laws to protect their citizens and their policies from federal meddling. All of us who are in the business of holding leaders accountable must redouble our efforts to defend the truth from his cynical assaults.

The United States is not a perfect country, and it has a great distance to go before it fully achieves its goals of liberty and equality. But preserving what works and defending the rules and values on which democracy depends are a shared responsibility. Everybody has a role to play in this drama.

WHY
TRUMP
LIES

Donald Trump did not invent the lie and is not even its master. Lies have oozed out of the White House for more than two centuries and out of politicians' mouths—out of all people's mouths—likely as long as there has been human speech.

But amid all those lies, told to ourselves and to one another in order to amass power, woo lovers, hurt enemies and shield ourselves against the often glaring discomfort of reality, humanity has always had an abiding respect for truth.

In the United States, born and periodically reborn out of the repeated recognition and rejection of the age-old lie that some people are meant to take dominion over others, truth is as vital a part of the civic, social and intellectual culture as justice and liberty. Our civilization is premised on the conviction that such a thing as truth exists, that it is knowable, that it is verifiable, that it exists independently of authority or popularity and that at some point—and preferably sooner rather than later—it will prevail.

Even American leaders who lie generally know the difference between their statements and the truth. Richard Nixon said "I am not a crook" but by that point must have seen that he was. Bill Clinton said "I did not have sexual relations with that woman" but knew that he did.

The insult that Donald Trump brings to the equation is an apparent disregard for fact so profound as to suggest that he may not see much practical distinction between lies, if he believes they serve him, and the truth.

His approach succeeds because of his preternaturally deft grasp of his audience. Though he is neither terribly articulate nor a seasoned politician, he has a remarkable instinct for discerning which conspiracy theories in which quasi-news source, or which of his own inner musings, will turn into ratings gold. He targets the darkness, anger and insecurity that hide in each of us and harnesses them for his own purposes. If one of his lies doesn't work—well, then he lies about that.

If we harbor latent racism or if we fear terror attacks by Muslim extremists, then he elevates a rumor into a public debate: Was Barack Obama born in Kenya, and is he therefore not really president?

An 'extremely credible source' has called my office and told me that @BarackObama's birth certificate is a fraud.

—Donald J. Trump (@realDonaldTrump)
August 6, 2012

"He targets the darkness, anger and insecurity that hide in each of us and harnesses them for his own purposes."

> Libya is being taken over by Islamic radicals–with @BarackObama's open support.
>
> —Donald J. Trump (**@realDonaldTrump**)
> August 31, 2011

If his own ego is threatened—if broadcast footage and photos show a smaller-sized crowd at his inauguration than he wanted—then he targets the news media, falsely charging outlets with disseminating "fake news" and insisting, against all evidence, that he has proved his case ("We caught them in a beauty," he said).

If his attempt to limit the number of Muslim visitors to the U.S. degenerates into an absolute fiasco and a display of his administration's incompetence, then he falsely asserts that terrorist attacks are underreported. (One case in point offered by the White House was the 2015 attack in San Bernardino, which in fact received intensive worldwide news coverage. The *Los Angeles Times* won a Pulitzer Prize for its reporting on the subject.)

If he detects that his audience may be wearying of his act, or if he worries about a probe into Russian meddling in the election that put him in office, he tweets in the middle of the night the astonishingly absurd claim that President Obama tapped his phones. And when evidence fails to support him he dispatches his aides to explain that by "phone tapping" he obviously didn't mean phone tapping. Instead of backing down when confronted with reality, he insists that his rebutted assertions will be vindicated as true at some point in the future.

Trump's easy embrace of untruth can sometimes be entertaining, in the vein of a Moammar Kadafi speech to the United Nations or the self-serving blathering of a six-year-old.

But he is not merely amusing. He is dangerous. His choice of falsehoods and his method of spewing them—often in tweets, as if he spent his days and nights glued to his bedside radio and was periodically set off by some drivel uttered by a talk show host who repeated something he'd read on some fringe blog—are a clue to Trump's thought processes and perhaps his lack of agency. He gives every indication that he is as much the gullible tool of liars as he is the liar in chief.

He has made himself the stooge, the mark, for every crazy blogger, political quack, racial theorist, foreign leader or nutcase peddling a story that he might repackage to his benefit as a tweet, an appointment, an executive order or a policy. He is a stranger to the concept of verification, the insistence on evidence and the standards of proof that apply in a court-room or a medical lab—and that ought to pre-vail in the White House.

There have always been those who accept the intellectually bankrupt notion that people are entitled to invent their own facts—consider the "9/11 was an inside job" trope—but

"He gives every indication that he is as much the gullible tool of liars as he is the liar in chief."

Trump's ascent marks the first time that the culture of alternative reality has made its home at 1600 Pennsylvania Avenue.

If Americans are unsure which Trump they have—the Machiavellian negotiator who lies to manipulate simpler minds, or one of those simpler minds himself—does it really matter? In either case he puts the nation in danger by undermining the role of truth in public discourse and policymaking, as well as the notion of truth being verifiable and mutually intelligible.

In the months ahead, Trump will bring his embrace of alternative facts on the nation's behalf into talks with China, North Korea or any number of powers with interests counter to ours and that constitute an existential threat. At home, Trump now becomes the embodiment of the populist notion (with roots planted at least as deeply in the Left as the Right) that verifiable truth is merely a concept invented by fusty intellectuals, and that popular leaders can provide some equally valid substitute. We've seen people like that before, and we have a name for them: demagogues.

Our civilization is defined in part by the disciplines—science, law, journalism—that have developed systematic methods to arrive at the truth. Citizenship brings with it the obligation to engage in a similar process. Good citizens test assumptions, question leaders, argue details, research claims.

Investigate. Read. Write. Listen. Speak. Think. Be wary of those who disparage the investigators, the readers, the writers, the listeners, the speakers and the thinkers. Be suspicious of those who confuse reality with reality TV, and those who repeat falsehoods while insisting, against all evidence, that they are true. To defend freedom, demand fact.

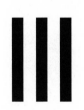

TRUMP'S AUTHORITARIAN VISION

Standing before the cheering throngs at the Republican National Convention in the summer of 2016, Donald Trump bemoaned how special interests had rigged the country's politics and its economy, leaving Americans victimized by unfair trade deals, incompetent bureaucrats and spineless leaders.

He swooped into politics, he declared, to subvert the powerful and rescue those who cannot defend themselves. "Nobody knows the system better than me, which is why I alone can fix it."

To Trump's faithful, those words were a rallying cry. But his critics heard something far more menacing in them: a dangerously authoritarian vision of the presidency—one that would crop up time and again as he talked about overruling generals, disregarding international law, ordering soldiers to commit war crimes, jailing his opponent.

Trump has no experience in politics; he's never previously run for office or held a government position. So perhaps he was unaware that one of the hallmarks of the American system of government is that the president's power to "fix" things unilaterally is constrained by an array of strong institutions—including the courts, the media, the permanent federal bureaucracy and Congress. Combined, they provide an essential defense against an imperial presidency.

Yet in his first weeks at the White House, President Trump has already sought to undermine many of those institutions. Those that have displayed the temerity to throw some hurdle in the way of a Trump objective have quickly felt the heat.

Consider Trump's feud with the courts.

He has repeatedly questioned the impartiality and the motives of judges. For example, he attacked the jurists who ruled against his order excluding travelers from seven majority Muslim nations, calling one a "so-called judge" and later tweeting:

> Just cannot believe a judge would put our country in such peril. If something happens blame him and court system. People pouring in. Bad!
>
> —Donald J. Trump (@realDonaldTrump)
> February 5, 2017

It's nothing new for presidents to disagree with court decisions. But Trump's direct, personal attacks on judges' integrity and on the legitimacy of the judicial system itself—and his irresponsible suggestion that the judiciary should be blamed for future terrorist attacks—go further. They aim to undermine public faith in the third branch of government.

The courts are the last line of defense for the Constitution and the rule of law; that's what makes them such a powerful buffer against an authoritarian leader. The president of the United States should understand that and respect it.

Other institutions under attack include:

1. **The electoral process.** Faced with certified election results showing that Hillary Clinton outpolled him by nearly 3 million votes, Trump repeated the unsubstantiated—and likely crackpot—assertion that Clinton's supporters had duped local polling places with millions of fraudulent votes. In a democracy, the right to vote is the one check that the people themselves hold against their leaders; sowing distrust in elections is the kind of thing leaders do when they don't want their power checked.

2. **The intelligence community.** After reports emerged that the Central Intelligence Agency believed Russia had tried to help Trump win, the president-elect's transition team responded: "These are the same people that said Saddam Hussein had weapons of mass destruction." It was a snarky, dismissive, undermining response—and the administration has continued to belittle the intelligence community and question its motives since then, while also leaking stories about possibly paring and restructuring its ranks. It is bizarre to watch Trump continue to tussle publicly with this particular part of the government, whose leaders he himself has appointed, as if he were still an outsider candidate raging against the machine. It's unnerving too, given the intelligence services' crucial role in protecting the country against hidden risks, assisting the U.S. military and helping inform Trump's decisions.

3. **The media.** Trump has blistered the mainstream media for reporting that has cast him in a poor light, saying outlets concocted narratives based on nonexistent anonymous sources. In February 2017 he said that the "fake news" media will "never represent the people," adding ominously: "And we're going to do something about it." His goal seems to be to defang the media watchdog by making the public doubt any coverage that accuses Trump of blundering or abusing his power.

4. **Federal agencies.** In addition to calling for agency budgets to be chopped by up to thirty percent, Trump appointed a string of cabinet secretaries who were hostile to much of their agencies' missions and the laws they're responsible for enforcing. He has also proposed deep cuts in federal research programs, particularly in those related to climate change. It's easier to argue that climate change isn't real when you're no longer collecting the data that documents it.

———

In a way, Trump represents a culmination of trends that have been years in the making.

Conservative talk radio hosts have long blasted federal judges as "activists" and regulators as meddlers in the economy, while advancing the myth of rampant election fraud. And gridlock in Washington has led previous presidents to try new ways to circumvent the checks on their power—witness President George W. Bush's use of signing statements to invalidate parts of bills Congress passed, and President Obama's aggressive use of executive orders when lawmakers balked at his proposals.

What's uniquely threatening about Trump's approach, though, is how many fronts he's

"He sees himself as not merely a force for change, but as a wrecking ball."

opened in this struggle for power and the vehemence with which he seeks to undermine the institutions that don't go along.

It's one thing to complain about a judicial decision or to argue for less regulation, but to the extent that Trump weakens public trust in essential institutions like the courts and the media, he undermines faith in democracy and in the system and processes that make it work.

Trump betrays no sense of the president's place among the myriad of institutions in the continuum of governance. He seems willing to violate long-established political norms without a second thought, and he cavalierly rejects the civility and deference that allow the system to run smoothly. He sees himself as not merely a force for change, but as a wrecking ball.

Will Congress act as a check on Trump's worst impulses as he moves forward? One test is the House and Senate intelligence committees' investigation into Russia's meddling in the presidential election; lawmakers need to muster the courage to follow the trail wherever it leads. Can the courts stand up to Trump? Already, several federal judges have issued rulings against the president's travel ban. And although Trump has railed against the decisions, he has obeyed them.

None of these institutions are eager to cede authority to the White House and they won't do so without a fight. It would be unrealistic to suggest that America's most basic democratic institutions are in imminent jeopardy.

But we should not view them as invulnerable either. Remember that Trump's verbal assaults are directed at the public, and are designed to chip away at people's confidence in these institutions and deprive them of their validity. When a dispute arises, whose actions are you going to consider legitimate? Whom are you going to trust? That's why the public has to be wary of Trump's attacks on the courts, the "deep state," the "swamp." We can't afford to be talked into losing our faith in the forces that protect us from an imperial presidency.

IV

TRUMP'S
WAR
ON JOURNALISM

In Donald Trump's America, the mere act of reporting news unflattering to the president is held up as evidence of bias. Journalists are slandered as "enemies of the people."

Facts that contradict Trump's version of reality are dismissed as "fake news." Reporters and their news organizations are "pathetic," "very dishonest," "failing," and even, in one memorable turn of phrase, "a pile of garbage."

Trump is, of course, not the first American president to whine about the news media or try to influence coverage. President George W. Bush saw the press as elitist and "slick." President Obama's press operation tried to exclude Fox News reporters from interviews, blocked many officials from talking to journalists and, most troubling, prosecuted more national security whistle-blowers and leakers than all previous presidents combined.

But Trump being Trump, he has escalated the traditionally adversarial relationship in demagogic and potentially dangerous ways.

Most presidents, irritated as they may have been, have continued to acknowledge—at least publicly—that an independent press plays an essential role in American democracy. They've recognized that while no news organization is perfect, honest reporting holds leaders and institutions accountable; that's why a free press was singled out for protection in the First Amendment and why outspoken, unfettered journalism is considered a hallmark of a free country.

Trump doesn't seem to buy it. On his very first day in office, he called journalists "among the most dishonest human beings on earth."

Since then he has regularly condemned legitimate reporting as "fake news." His administration has blocked mainstream news organizations, including *The Times*, from briefings and his secretary of state chose to travel to Asia without taking the press corps, breaking a longtime tradition.

This may seem like bizarre behavior from a man who consumes the news in print and on television so voraciously and who is in many ways a *product* of the media. He comes from reality TV, from talk radio with Howard Stern, from the gossip pages of the New York City tabloids, for whose columnists he was both a regular subject and a regular source.

But Trump's strategy is pretty clear: By branding reporters as liars, he apparently hopes to discredit, disrupt or bully into silence anyone who challenges his version of reality. By undermining trust in news organizations and delegitimizing journalism and muddling the facts so that Americans no longer know who to believe, he can deny and distract and help push his administration's far-fetched storyline.

"He apparently hopes to discredit, disrupt or bully into silence anyone who challenges his version of reality."

It's a cynical strategy, with some creepy overtones. For instance, when he calls journalists "enemies of the people," Trump (whether he knows it or not) echoes Josef Stalin and other despots.

But it's an effective strategy. Such attacks are politically expedient at a moment when trust in the news media is as low as it's ever been, according to Gallup. And they're especially resonant with Trump's supporters, many of whom see journalists as part of the swamp that needs to be drained.

Of course, we're not perfect. Some readers find news organizations too cynical; others say we're too elitist. Some say we downplay important stories, or miss them altogether. Conservatives often perceive an unshakable liberal bias in the media (while critics on the Left see big, corporate-owned media institutions like *The Times* as hopelessly centrist).

To do the best possible job, and to hold the confidence of the public in turbulent times, requires constant self-examination and evolution. Soul-searching moments—such as those that occurred after the *New York Times* was criticized for its coverage of the Bush administration and the Iraq war or, more recently, when the media failed to take Trump's candidacy seriously enough in the early days of his campaign—can help us do a better job for readers. Even if we are not faultless, the news media remain an essential component in the democratic process and should not be undermined by the president.

Some critics have argued that if Trump is going to treat the news media like the "opposition party" (a phrase his senior aide Steve Bannon has used), then journalists should start acting like opponents too. But that would be a mistake. The role of an institution like the *Los Angeles Times* (or the *New York Times*, the *Wall Street Journal* or CNN) is to be independent and aggressive in pursuit of the truth—not to take sides. The editorial pages are the exception: Here we can and should express our opinions about Trump. But the news pages, which operate separately, should report intensively without prejudice, partiality or partisanship.

Given the very real dangers posed by this administration, we should be indefatigable in covering Trump, but shouldn't let his bullying attitude persuade us to be anything other than objective, fair, open-minded and dogged.

The fundamentals of journalism are more important than ever. With the president of the United States launching a direct assault on the integrity of the mainstream media, news organizations, including the *Los Angeles Times*, must be courageous in our reporting and resolute in our pursuit of the truth.

V

CONSPIRACY
THEORIST
IN CHIEF

It was bad enough back in 2011 when Donald Trump began peddling the crackpot conspiracy theory that President Barack Obama was not a native-born American. But at least Trump was just a private citizen then.

By the time he tweeted in March 2017 that Obama had sunk so low as to "tapp [sic] my phones during the very sacred election process," Trump was a sitting president accusing a predecessor of what would have been an impeachable offense.

Trump went public with this absurd accusation without consulting the law enforcement and intelligence officials who would have disabused him of a conspiracy theory he apparently imbibed from right-wing media. After the FBI director debunked it, Trump held fast, claiming he hadn't meant that he had been literally wiretapped.

Most people know by now that the new president of the United States traffics in untruths and half-truths, and that his word cannot be taken at face value.

Even more troubling, though, is that much of his misinformation is of the creepiest kind. Implausible conspiracy theories from fly-by-night websites; unsubstantiated speculations from supermarket tabloids. Bigoted stories he may have simply made up; stuff he heard on TV talk shows.

The concept of global warming was created by and for the Chinese in order to make U.S. manufacturing non-competitive.

—Donald J. Trump (@realDonaldTrump)
November 6, 2012

> In addition to winning the Electoral College in a landslide, I won the popular vote if you deduct the millions of people who voted illegally
>
> —Donald J. Trump (@realDonaldTrump)
> November 27, 2016

This is pathetic, but it's also alarming. If Trump feels free to take to Twitter to make wild, paranoid, unsubstantiated accusations against his predecessor, why should the nation believe what he says about a North Korean missile test, Russian troop movements in Europe or a natural disaster in the United States?

Trump's willingness to embrace unproven, conspiratorial and even racist theories became clear during the campaign, when he repeatedly told tall tales that seemed to reinforce ugly stereotypes about minorities. Take his now famous assertion that he watched thousands of people in "a heavy Arab population"

"He is allowing the credibility of his unimaginably powerful office to be exploited and wasted on crackpot ideas."

in New Jersey cheer the collapse of the World Trade Center on 9/11, an astonishing account that no one has been able to verify. PolitiFact rated that as "Pants on Fire."

Or his retweeting of a bogus crime statistic purporting to show that eighty-one percent of white homicide victims are killed by blacks. (The correct figure was fifteen percent.)

On several occasions he retweeted white nationalists. (Remember the image of Hillary Clinton and the Star of David, for instance?)

His engagement with, to put it politely, out-of-the-mainstream ideas has attracted some strange bedfellows. It may not be fair to attribute to his senior aide, Steve Bannon, all the views that were published on the controversial alt-right site Breitbart.com, of which Bannon was the executive chairman. But it is certainly fair to wonder why Trump has elevated to a senior West Wing position a man who has trafficked in nonsense, bigotry and rank speculation.

Of course it was widely hoped that when Trump came into office he would put the conspiracy theories and red-meat scare stories behind him. Perhaps the "lock her up" mantra and the fear-mongering about Mexican rapists and the racial dog whistles and the assertions about Ted Cruz's father's connection to Lee Harvey Oswald—perhaps all that was just part of a cynical bid for votes, and it would go away when the election was over.

But there's no sign of that. Trump seems as willing to mouth off today as he was on the campaign—about wiretaps, inauguration crowds, fraudulent voters, you name it. And the problem with that is that he is no longer a blowhard TV personality or a raunchy guest on Howard Stern or a self-promoting real estate magnate or even a long-shot candidate for the Republican nomination. He's now the president of the United States, and he is allowing the credibility of his unimaginably powerful office to be exploited and wasted on crackpot ideas that have been rightly discredited by politicians from both parties.

VI

CALIFORNIA FIGHTS BACK

When Donald Trump threatened on the campaign trail to deport every single immigrant living in the country illegally, bring back offshore drilling and reverse the anti-pollution policies that help clear smoggy skies, Californians immediately understood that our state would be disproportionately affected—and disproportionately harmed—by the reckless policies he was hoping to enact.

After he was sworn in, he went further, singling out the state for attack. "California," Trump declared in February 2017, "in many ways is out of control." In one overwrought tweet, he suggested that the federal government should cut all funding for UC Berkeley because a protest against a conservative guest speaker had turned violent. A few days later, he declared—even more irresponsibly—that he would "defund" the entire state if he felt it wasn't cooperating sufficiently with his efforts to root out undocumented immigrants.

Trump had already alienated many state voters with his plans to build a costly and unnecessary border wall, revoke the health insurance of millions of low-income people and gut climate-change policies. Now, he was taking on California itself, a state in which more than one out of ten Americans live, and which sends more than $350 billion to Washington each year in federal taxes (and gets substantially less than that back). A state with strong progressive values that it will not happily see undermined.

To express their dissatisfaction, hundreds of thousands of people gathered at rallies in the state's major cities. One man's quixotic California secession campaign became a cause célèbre. And California's political leaders vowed to fight back.

Governor Jerry Brown grumbled that if Trump cut climate data-gathering efforts, California would launch its "own damn satellite." Legislators put former U.S. Attorney General Eric Holder on a hefty retainer to help challenge Trump's initiatives in court even before he'd announced any. They filed a mountain of bills reacting to an array of reprehensible policies that the new president was thought to be considering. "We're going to do what we need to do to protect the people of California," said state Attorney General Xavier Becerra.

The initial response of state leaders—which included some good ideas along with a bit of flailing and a touch of panic—was understandable given the enormity of the threat. But as we settle in for the next four years, California needs to be clear-eyed about the challenges it faces and strategic about how it responds. An all-out war with the federal government is neither sustainable nor wise. The state will have to choose its battles.

"An all-out war with the federal government is neither sustainable nor wise. The state will have to choose its battles."

For starters, California should continue to pursue its agenda on human and civil rights, on clean air, water and climate change, and on equality. Trump can dismantle the federal Clean Power Plan, but he can't stop the state from moving toward its renewable energy goal of fifty percent by 2030 as laid out in SB 350 two years ago. The U.S. Environmental Protection Agency can reduce national fuel efficiency standards, but if it seeks to revoke California's waiver that lets the state set its own, tougher rules, state lawmakers should fight back, including taking the agency to court if necessary. Trump can continue his counterproductive and mean-spirited efforts to deport non-criminal immigrants living in the country illegally, but the state's local law enforcement agencies are not legally required to do the feds' job for them; they should not.

California's political leaders should reach out to other states—including red ones— to develop alliances on issues of common concern. Trump's contempt for renewable energy resources, the reform of marijuana laws and the expansion of Medicaid, for instance, will surely alienate officials in other state capitols. Smoggy skies aren't unique to Los Angeles, and western states have already shown interest in investing in renewable energy.

However, California lawmakers must also be careful about allowing the "resist at all costs" mentality to push them further than they ought to go.

Consider the biggest California vs. Trump fight so far: immigration. It is true that local police and sheriff's deputies should not be turned into immigration agents, doing work that properly belongs to the federal government and which would hamper their ability to work effectively with immigrant communities. But neither should the state, in its zeal to resist Trump, throw up obstacles to cooperation that would protect serious criminals from deportation. Early versions of SB 54—the so-called sanctuary state bill that would spell out how local police agencies should work with Immigration and Customs Enforcement agents—allowed the state to make policing decisions that have traditionally been made locally, could have goaded ICE agents into even more harmful immigration sweeps and, potentially, made it harder to keep violent criminals off the streets.

Many Californians are extremely—and rationally—pessimistic about the next few years under President Trump. But here's another hard truth: If and when there are opportunities for reasonable collaboration with the new administration, the state must be prepared to take them. California relies on the federal government for $105 billion in aid each year, money it badly needs. Total noncooperation is not an option. Besides, Sacramento and Washington, D.C., have certain mutual interests: If the president wants shovel-ready infrastructure projects to fund, we have plenty.

"California is an integral part of the United States, where it should remain, staying actively engaged."

That means keeping open the lines of communication, as both Governor Brown and Los Angeles Mayor Eric Garcetti seem eager to do. With luck, Trump will in turn recognize that the state's big industries—tech, agriculture, entertainment, tourism—are immensely important to the national economy. If California suffers at the hands of Trump's policies, so will the rest of the nation.

The reality is that California cannot go it alone. Let's stop fantasizing about "Calexit." As fun as it may be to imagine California taking its giant, job-creating, climate-protecting, immigrant-friendly economy and building its own nation, history suggests that would be neither wise nor feasible. California is an integral part of the United States, where it should remain, staying actively engaged.

In the days ahead, we Californians must stand up to protect our nation and defend our state. We must read, write and protest. Attend meetings and speak out honestly to those in power. We must vote. Not just for president, but for school board as well. Stand up for the rule of law and the democratic process while also opposing the dangerous policies of America's new leader.

For the next four years, we must cooperate when it is possible, but fight back when it is necessary in the interests of our state and the union to which it belongs.

Acknowledgments

Special thanks are due to a number of people who were invaluable in making this project succeed. Steve Wasserman, the publisher and executive director of Heyday, approached us about collecting the articles for a book and helped shepherd it to publication. Many people helped in the creation and publication of the original articles in the *Los Angeles Times*, including Wesley Bausmith, Judy Cramer, Matthew Fleischer, Megan Garvey, Lorena Iniguez, Hillary Manning, Alexandra Manzano, Andrea Roberson, Ben Welsh, Michael Whitley and Annie Yu.

About the Author

Founded in 1881, the *Los Angeles Times* is the largest news-gathering organization west of the Mississippi. Now read by more than 50 million unique visitors monthly, *The Times'* journalism has won forty-four Pulitzer Prizes, six of which were gold medals for public service.

The editorials collected in this book are the work of *The Times'* editorial board, which is responsible for determining the positions of the paper on the important issues of the day. Unlike articles written by the paper's reporters in its news pages, editorials are works of opinion. They are unsigned because they represent the consensus of the board.

The opinions expressed in these editorials were reached through a process of discussion and deliberation by editorial writers Kerry

Cavanaugh, Mariel Garza, Robert Greene, Carla Hall, Karin Klein, Scott Martelle and Michael McGough, working with editorial page editor Nicholas Goldberg, deputy editor Jon Healey and editor-in-chief and publisher Davan Maharaj.

About the Publisher

Heyday is an independent, nonprofit 501(c)(3) publisher founded in 1974 in Berkeley, California. It promotes civic engagement and social justice, and celebrates California's natural beauty. Through books, public events and outreach programs, Heyday works to give voice to the voiceless and to realize the California dream of diversity and enfranchisement. In 2017, Heyday marked thirty years of publishing *News from Native California*, the state's leading magazine of Indian affairs and culture. Heyday seeks to build a vibrant community of writers and readers, activists and thinkers.

A Note on Type

Trump Mediaeval is named after Georg Trump, its designer, who created it between 1954 and 1962. An old-style serif typeface, it was used both by the C.E. Weber foundry as metal type and Linotype for hot metal typesetting. Its classical aspect recalls earlier Venetian typefaces and is commonly associated with books of enduring merit and bespoke design. Pleasing to the eye, it is a font of balance and serenity whose proportions and aesthetic appeal are widely admired by typographic connoisseurs the world over.